Skeletons in My Closet

Janice Claxton

Skeletons in My Closet

ISBN 978-1-947741-05-8

Kingdom Publishing, LLC
Odenton, MD 21113

Printed in the USA

ACKNOWLEDGEMENTS

The skeletons in my closet is my testimony of personal life events and I would like to acknowledge those persons who have been instrumental in helping me to organize my thoughts, protecting me and nurturing me, listening to my stories and empowering me to believe that I could accomplish writing my book. Most of all, I like to acknowledge the person who shared a lot of my experiences and memories.

To my husband Michael Claxton, thank you for loving me unconditionally no matter what baggage I brought into our marriage.

To my wonderful mother-in-law, Dr. Deborah J. Claxton, I really appreciate you reading my story and assisting me with organizing my thoughts.

To my daughter, Jessica Wongus, thank you for accepting my apology for some of things you had to live through.

To my son, Peter Anakaraonye, thank you for supporting me and not being embarrassed about me telling my story.

To my twin sister, Janet Addison, thank you for being there for me during the rough times in my life.

To my father (deceased), Julius Griffin, thank you for being a mother and a father to me; when I needed your love and affection you were always there for me.

Table of Contents

How It All Began

I have decided to tell my story because I no longer want to carry around the skeletons in my closet. Those things that keep you in bondage and keep you from living freely from all the issues you had to deal with in your past. The things that burden you and won't let you move on and become the successful person that you were born to be. Sometimes we cannot control what happens to us in our life, but it is important that we do not hold on to these things. You must hold on and keep pushing through your circumstances. If you give up now, you may never see what your end result may be. I can look back over my life and say that I am a stronger woman because of the things I endured while growing up.

Can you imagine your mother dying when you were just four years old? I remember that day because she was dressed up, she smelled so good, and she looked so pretty. My mom reached out to hug me and I remember being afraid of the mink fox that she wore around her neck. My mother told my twin sister and I that we could wait up for her to come home as she promised to return with cake for the both of us to eat. We were so excited we ran around the house and jumped and sang with joy and happiness. A few hours later there was a knock at the door. My 13-year-old sister answered the door and called for my dad to come downstairs as the police officer who was standing in the door requested to speak with him. I remember my dad leaving the house with the policeman and when he had returned to the house he was very sad and had been crying. He went to his chair, sat down and held his head. My older sister asked dad what was wrong and he told her what had happened to my mom. My mom had been hit by a car and killed. She started crying and I just looked at them both with no understanding of what was going on. My dad told my twin and I to come over to him and he told us that our mom had died and went to heaven. We clearly did not understand what my father had said because we began to jump up and down on the sofa singing mommy went to heaven. When my 17-year-old sister came home she was wondering why we were not in bed. We told her that mommy went to heaven. She looked at my dad for understanding and he told her the story. She ran out of the house in tears.

When I was growing up my family did not talk openly about death. It wasn't until a few years later that I started to really understand what it meant for someone to die. I began to resent my mom dying while I was so young because I could not run home and tell her about my day at school. I could not ask her what dress I should wear or even get a motherly hug. I pretended that she was still alive and I would save her a seat at the kitchen table just so that I could ask her all kinds of questions that I never received an answer to. When someone mentioned they were going to tell their mom about a situation I became very jealous and angry. This went on for quite a while. One day I asked my dad if I kept praying for mom to come see me would she visit me? Dad said yes. I had been praying for a very long time and she never came to visit me. I told dad that he was a liar and he just looked at me and said nothing at all.

One night while I was in bed dreaming about my mom I heard a voice say to me "open your eyes". I thought it was a dream but when I opened my eyes I saw my mom standing at the foot of my bed. She was dressed like an angel and I could see that it was her face in a silhouette type figure. I screamed so loud for my dad to turn on the light because of how scared I was. I could not believe my eyes. I jumped out of the bed and ran into my dad's room and told him what I saw. He just looked at me as if he was surprised to hear what had just happened. I told my dad that I did not want mom to come to see me again. I asked him if I prayed for her not to come again would she listen. Dad just nodded his head and told me to go back to sleep. I did not go back to my bed for several nights. My dad told me that I could not sleep with him and needed to go to my own bed. I told him to please keep the light on because I would not be able to sleep in the dark. I often wonder if my mom heard my prayer because I never saw her visit me again.

My dad met a Caucasian woman who moved in with us and he eventually married. She called my sister and I the gold dust twins. She seemed to be a little crazy. She would tell us to call her mom and then later she wanted us to call her by her name. One day I was in the kitchen washing dishes and she came over to me and handed me a knife. She told me to cut her with the knife and I began to cry because I was afraid of how she was acting. She was the worst step mother I could have lived with. She told my twin sister and I that we could go see the State Street parade around the corner from our house. We left to go to the parade and we were sitting on the sidewalk enjoying the parade. A police officer came over to us and asked us what our names were. We told him our names and he asked us to come with him. We were so embarrassed. He took us back home and we found out that our step mother had reported us as runaway twins. We tried to tell the policeman that we did not runaway but he did not believe us. This whole situation was very upsetting to me. My step mother tried to tell my dad the same story but I believe my dad was on to her craziness.

The next day my dad had to take us to work with him. His crazy wife told him that if he leaves us home with her, she was going to kill us. We enjoyed going to work with dad but he knew that we could not do this too often. He explained to us that he was going to have to get a babysitter. We were only 8 years old so we could not be left at home alone or even with his crazy wife. Eventually, my dad requested for a divorce from his wife because he learned that she had been in a mental institution for several years.

My baby sister lived right up the street from my house. My dad would send us to the sitter's house when he had to go to work. She was a very strange woman who had no kids of her own. Her husband was a weird guy who often requested to play Hide-in- Go Seek with my sister and I. He would stand directly behind me in the alley and hold me close to him while rubbing his body up against my buttocks. I would think to myself that there is definitely something wrong with what he is doing. He would always want to pick me up and hold me close to his body. I would ask him to put me down because I did not like what he was doing to me. I never told my dad because I felt as though I would get in trouble for letting him do these things to me. One day he tried to sit me on his lap and I tried to get away from him and his wife just sat there looking at what was going on and she never said a word to him. I got so tired of going to the baby sitter's house that I finally yelled at my dad and said I hate going to the sitter's house. Her husband always wants to pick me up and I don't like it. I saw the look on my dad's face as he walked quickly towards the front door and he left out of the house. I am not sure what all happened but my sister and I never returned to that sitter's house again.

Another time I was upstairs on the third floor of our house and I heard a knock at my bedroom window. I looked and it was my neighbor standing at the window. He was about 21 years old and he asked me to open the window. Then he got on his knees and pulled down his pants. I could not believe what I was seeing. I felt an evil spirit come out of me and I lifted the window just a little. He told me to suck his penis so I told him to stick it in the window so that I could reach it. I had both of

5

my hands on the window frame and as he stuck his penis inside I quickly closed the window down on his penis and ran down stairs. I could hear him screaming as I continued to run away to get help. When I returned with my older sister he was gone. She told me to stop making up stories and I tried to tell her that I was telling the truth. Later we heard the ambulance siren coming in our neighborhood. They went into the house next door to us and we saw that it was the neighbor being taken out on a stretcher. My sister looked at me and I began to cry because I thought he was going to die. Several weeks went by and I saw him sitting on the steps and I acted like I did not know him. He just stared at me because he was trying to figure out if I was the twin who closed the window on him.

On another occasion, my dad, my sister, and I went to visit our aunt and uncle who lived in Maryland. They had a son and a daughter who were my cousins. My dad was playing cards in another room with family members. I was in the front room watching TV. My male cousin told me to come and sit down beside him so I did. He put his hand under my dress and played with my vagina. No one had ever done that before so I removed his hand. He pulled down his pants and asked me to suck his penis. I looked at him and told him no. I was 10 years old and I knew that it was wrong for him to do those things to me. I was afraid to tell because I felt that he would deny it. He was much older than me. That bothered me for a long time. Every time we would go to visit my aunt and uncle I would stay close to my dad. My aunt would always tell me to go play and let my dad have a break. If she only knew what her son had done to me maybe she would have left me alone. I remember praying to God that when I grew up I wanted to marry a man of God by the time I was 40 years old. I guess I felt that I would have an honest man in my life just like my dad.

My dad was a Catholic and he made my sister and I go to Mass every Sunday morning. We even had to go to Catholic school on Saturday and we really hated it. Most of the children were Caucasian and they treated us differently. The teachers and the students were very mean to us. One time my dad sent us to Mass early one Sunday morning and my sister and I chose not to go. Instead we went to the bakery and bought some donuts to eat. Later we returned home and my dad told us that our God parents told him that we did not come for Mass that morning. We tried to tell him that we went and then he asked us to show him the program. We were busted, so he told us that we had to go to the next Mass service. I was so angry for getting caught.

When I was about 12 years old my dad met a really nice Caucasian woman whom I loved so dearly. She came into my life at the right time. I needed a woman to teach me about womanhood; how to keep a house clean, cook and wash. This lady was God sent and we got along perfectly. She could cook and she taught me how to be clean and keep myself nice at all times. I could talk to her about anything and she would have an answer to anything I needed to know. She was just like a mother to me. Finally, I could come home from school and tell someone what my day was like and it really felt good. I had not been able to do this before and I was no longer angry about other girls telling me that they were going to go home and tell their mother about how things went in school that day. I never felt like she was Caucasian or I was Afro- American. I felt that color was not an issue, but how we treated one another was more important if we were going to have a healthy relationship.

I remember my dad telling my sister and I that we were going to be moving from Harrisburg, PA to Baltimore, MD. I was not happy about this decision at all because I would have to leave all my friends behind. I found out later that my dad wanted to move because he had experienced some racial issues. It was time to move and I could not accept the fact that I would be going to a new school and leaving all my friends behind. We arrived in Baltimore and I was trying to get over the fact that I may not see my friends again. I started to make new friend over the summer. It was time for school and my sister and I were in the same class for the first time. We had trouble responding to our new environment and we became very withdrawn.

Our teacher became very upset with us and requested to have a meeting with my dad. I really hated the new school and I did not want to socialize with anyone. I remember one time when the teacher called me to go to the blackboard to solve a math problem. I knew the answer but I did not want to go up in front of the classroom. My teacher demanded that I respond to his request. I got up out of my seat and walked very slow towards the front of the class. I heard a boy's voice say, "she is so stupid and weird acting". This made me very angry and I wanted to tell him to mind his own business. I was in the 7th grade, I was in front of the class, and I did not know anyone. I felt the students staring at me while I was writing the answer on the board. Once I finished I quickly went back to my seat to sit down. I rolled my eyes at the boy who was saying mean things about me and then I gave him the middle finger. He got so mad that he yelled across the room to me "your mother". I must have lost my mind because I jumped out of my seat and walked over to his seat. I was going to punch him in his face but someone stopped me. He jumped up out of his seat and reached around the person that was holding me back and he hit me in my arm. I broke loose and we began to fight in the classroom. I remember the teacher standing in between us but I did not care. I had to hit him back and when I did the teacher pushed me back and slammed the boy up against the blackboard. He charged towards me and we started to fight again. I felt his hand hitting me in my stomach and I grabbed his hand so that I could bite him.

I did not know that it was my teacher's hand that I was biting and it caused the teacher to yell, "who just bit me"? I knew it was me but I said to the teacher that I don't bite. The teacher was angry and in so much pain that he pushed the boy away from him and blamed him for his finger getting bit. I was so afraid that he would find out the truth so I remained quiet and stuck with my story. The teacher took us to the office and our parents were called to come to the school. We got suspended for two days and the boy's parents got stuck with a medical bill. I really felt bad about it but he should not have picked with me.

Off to Jersey

It was summer break and my older sisters wanted us to come visit them in New Jersey for the summer. My sister and I had never been away from my dad before but since it was family we were excited to go. My dad initially said no but my sister and I convinced him to let us go.

We had two older siblings living in New Jersey so we decided to split our visit between the two of them. My sisters were Muslims at the time and we began practicing it too. They let us dress in long garments and head wraps. We stopped eating pork because of all the stories we were told about how unhealthy it was.

One night I was asleep in the top bunk bed and my sister's boyfriend came into the room and he tried to rape me. I did not like the way he looked at me when we first met so I did not say much around him. My twin sister felt the same way. He kept trying to pull down my shorts that I had underneath of my night gown. I had learned to put a pin inside of my zipper to keep it from sliding down and coming open. I pretended to be sleep hoping that he would leave me alone and go away. Finally, I opened my eyes and said, "STOP it!!" I said it very loud and he ran out of the room. In the morning when my sister and her boyfriend left for work, I called my other sister and requested for her to come and take my sister and I to her house. We did not feel comfortable staying any longer. I explained to my sister what had happened and requested that she never tell anyone. I believe she mentioned it to my sister because she was very upset with me. I knew that I didn't do anything to provoke what happened to me so I just let it go.

While we were in New Jersey my sister and I were introduced to marijuana and we started smoking it almost every morning. It was finally time to go back home but since we had so much fun we asked dad if we could return next summer and he said we could. We told dad that we never wanted to eat pork again. He said that we were born and raised eating it and there was nothing wrong with eating pork. Since I did most of the cooking and my sister washed the clothes, when I would go to the market to buy food I made sure to never buy any pork.

My High School Experiences

I was in high school now and I met a lot of new friends. I was excited about my new school and I was an honor student in the A course program. My sister, my cousin and I all were in the same class and we studied together all the time. I joined the Pep Squad team and I was on the track team. I ran so fast that I received awards for the 440 relays, 220 yard dash and 100 yard dash. I knew I had a great career ahead of me as a track star. I practiced all the time and loved to run.

One day my sister, my cousin and I were playing in the hallway at school on the steps. I remember a classmate had joined us in the hallway and said that she remembered one of us jumping down all the steps. I looked at the steps and said that it was not me but that I was willing to try it. There were about 14 or more steps and that appeared to be very wide and long. I jumped down all the steps and everyone was very shocked that I made it. I tried it again and this time I landed on the last step and twisted my left knee. I heard it pop and I was in so much pain. I asked someone to please go get me some help. Everyone looked at me and said stop playing girl you are ok. I began to cry and they all knew that I was serious. I begged them not to mention that I jumped down the steps because I knew I was going to get in trouble for doing such a foolish thing. The gym teacher and nurse arrived and they examined me. I could not move my left leg and it was very swollen. The ambulance arrived and they placed me on the stretcher. I heard a discussion about me falling down the steps and that I had on tennis shoes that may have caused me to slip. I was in pain and crying while I was being transported through the hallways of the school. I was embarrassed because all the students were staring at me. I arrived at the hospital and my dad was already there waiting for me. I was examined and told that I had torn ligaments in my knee and had a contusion. My leg was braced and I was given crutches to use to get around. I just wanted to go home and get into bed. I was out of school for a few weeks. My boyfriend would call me during the day to check on me. When I returned to school I was given an elevator key to get to and from my classes. My boyfriend would carry my books for me and my sister would tease him and call him the little helper boy. He would get so mad at her and I would to.

One day I asked some of my friends that had been laughing at my sister's jokes to ride to class on the elevator along with me. Everyone was so excited to get on the elevator with me. I pushed the button that took us to the roof. Once the doors open we were all impressed at how much snow was on the roof and I asked them to go look over the roof to see what was there. Everyone got off and I quickly closed the doors. I could hear them yelling for me to open the doors because it was getting cold. I left them up on the roof and got off on the second floor so that I could go to my class. I sent the elevator back up on the roof to get them. I was afraid that they would tell on me but no one did. They were all mad at me and did not speak to me for a while.

My boyfriend and I would always leave snacks in each other's locker. We were the best of friends and we never talked about having sex. His mother was a single mom and they lived in public housing. He would miss a lot of school so that he could go to work to help his mom financially. I would go in my deep freezer and take out meats to give his mom to cook. She would always ask me if I was sure that it was ok for her to take the meats. My dad would never miss it because I did all the cooking in the house. My friend and his mom were such nice people; I just wanted to help them out. I was 17 years old and I realized that a lot of girls wanted to be with my boyfriend because he was the finest guy in the school. He was nice, sexy and could dress nice. He was also very smart and always passed his exams even though he missed a lot of time from school.

One day I pretended to be pregnant by him to make the girls jealous. We had never had sex before so he knew that it was not true. I told him to go along with my story and I coached him on what to say if he was questioned. I gave him a baby picture of my niece to show if he needed to verify our story. I would wear a large shirt over my pants to make the story seem true. I made it appear as if I did not stay home for my entire maternity leave and the girls were so mad that he had a baby with me. We pretended to have a little girl and she was so cute.

One day my boyfriend asked me if I was ready to have sex and I told him that I was not on any birth control. I told him that I wanted to get protected first and then we could have sex. I made him wait for another 6 months because I really did not want to have sex. I was still a virgin and afraid. I told him to come to my house after school one day because I knew what time my dad would be coming home from work. He was trying to be easy with me but it was too uncomfortable for me. Before we knew it my dad was home and I could hear him downstairs. I was so afraid that we were going to get caught. I told my boyfriend to get dressed while I went downstairs to figure out a way for him to escape without my dad seeing him. My dad was heading for the bathroom down stairs so I started a conversation with him. After he went into the bathroom I locked the outside door and ran upstairs to tell my boyfriend to hurry up and come down. I heard my dad saying unlock the door and I told him that I was coming to let him out. My boyfriend ran down the steps and out the front door. I went to unlock the bathroom door and my dad wanted to know why I locked him in the bathroom. I told him that I was just playing with him and gave him a big hug. He told me not to do that again and I told him that I was sorry. I was afraid to try that again in my house so the next time we went to my boyfriend's house.

It all happened so quickly. I was walking to the store and decided to take a short cut through a playground area. A man said something to me but I didn't hear what he said so I kept on walking. He walked over to where I was and asked me what my name was. I softly said my name and started to walk away. He was tall, slim, and very attractive but I had no interest at the time. I was 17 years old, very quiet and reserved.

Another time I was on my way to the playground to tell my nieces to come home for dinner and the same man was standing outside again on the playground staring at me so I said hello to him. The man remembered my name and started to ask me questions about myself and I answered just a few before it was time to leave. He gave me his number and stated that he would like to get to know me better. I took the number and said goodbye. Before I left, I heard a voice say, "Leave that young girl alone because you are too old for her". I continued to walk along with my little nieces and we went home. Later I called the man's number and he did not answer so I left him a message to return my call.

In a few days, it was going to be my senior prom and I was so excited to go. I walked to the playground and sat on the swings while my nieces played for a while outside. I saw the man coming towards me so I stopped my swing so that I could communicate with him. He told me that he got my message and he wanted to take me out to dinner one day. I remember my heart beating a mile a minute because I could see how handsome he looked that day. I could not imagine him being interested in me or even wanting to go on a date with me. One thing I knew was that I would have to get permission from my dad, but that would not be easy. I said to myself how should I tell my dad because he may not let me go out with an older man.

I went to my prom with my high school boyfriend and we had a great time. I kept thinking about my new friend (the man) and it became a distraction for me at some point. Later I was ready to go home so that I could call the man friend.

As soon as I arrived home from the prom my dad was sitting on the porch waiting for me to get home. I went into the house and changed my clothes and then I called the man on the phone. He answered the phone and we talked for a while. I asked him how old he was and he never answered me directly. I told him that I did not date married men or a man who had kids. I told him I was 19 years old. Later that week I managed to get permission to go out to dinner but I did not tell my dad that it was someone he had not met.

We arrived at a restaurant and we ordered our food. I was a little afraid because I knew that I was not going to be able to stay out too late. I did not want to tell the man that I would have to leave soon. He ordered me a drink and I took a few sips and started to feel mellow and was not thinking much about going home. We left the restaurant and I ended up at his apartment. I started to become afraid because I really didn't know the man very well. I told him that I wanted to go home because my dad would be wondering where I was. He looked me in my eyes and began to hug and kiss me. I pulled away and demanded for him to take me home. He started saying things to me but I could not hear what he was saying. He grabbed his keys and walked towards the door and I followed him to the car. We never said a word as he drove me to my door. I got out of the car and walked away from the car in silence because I was so ashamed of how I acted.

A week went by and I did not hear from the man. I was wondering what he was thinking about but I was not going to contact him. Later that week I returned to the playground to pick up my nieces and I saw the man walking towards me. He stopped me and asked me why I acted so afraid of him and that he was not going to hurt me. I told him that I did not know why I acted the way I did. He smiled at me and said that it was ok. We talked for a while as I waited for my nieces to play at the playground.

I knew that it was time for me to be honest with my boyfriend and let him know that I was seeing someone else. He would always be a special person in my life but I did not want to cheat on him. He agreed that we would see other people so that I could see what I really wanted in a relationship. I really felt bad but I knew he would not have a problem getting another girlfriend. I was seeing an older man and I was in my own world. I had never seen hair on a man's chest and I thought that it was very sexy. He would leave his shirt unbuttoned and I could see it on his chest. He also had a car to drive and that was important to me.

One evening the man and I talked about me going over to his apartment. By that time, I was the legal age of 18 and I felt like my dad would not mind me going out for an overnight date. The man came to my house to pick me up for a date and my dad requested his phone number before I could go out with him. We left and we went to his apartment. I remembered how I felt the first time I was there, but I tried not thinking about it because I was becoming scared of what may happen to me. I was infatuated with being with an older man, but also afraid of having sex with him.

We went into the bedroom and I could feel my heart beating faster and faster. As I was taking off my clothes, I was watching my friend undress and I was amazed at his manhood. He began kissing me and laid me on the bed. He got on top of me and as I felt him enter my body it was not what I expected. It hurt and I felt uncomfortable because he was grinding on me so hard. He looked at my face and immediately stopped and asked me if I was ok. I said yes even though I was not. He was a stranger to me and I did not want him to view me a certain way if I told him I couldn't take it. Afterwards I tried to go to sleep to forget about it but then his phone rang. It was my dad on the phone. My dad was yelling and saying for him to bring me home and asked what was he doing that would take all night? My friend hung up the phone and told me to get dress because my dad said that I had to come home.

Deception! Deception!

I remember being in college and I had a math teacher who asked me to stay after class for a discussion. I realized that he did not want to talk about my grades instead he asked me personal questions. I could not understand why it was important for him to find out if I was married. I answered no and then started to walk away. The next day I had my final exam and I was prepared for it because I had an A average going into the final exam. It was summer break for me and I was preparing myself for a trip to Florida with my family. I received a phone call from my college teacher asking me if I liked the grade that I had received. I did not know what he was talking about so I explained to him that I did not receive my grade in the mail. He stated that if I did not like my grade I could discuss it with him. I was upset because I was not clear about his intentions. Later after I returned from my vacation I opened my mail to see my grades. Oh no, I received a D in my math class. I thought to myself something is wrong because I understood everything on my exam. I had a hard time believing what I was seeing.

A few days later I received another phone call from my math teacher and I was eager to hear what he had to say about my failing grade. He stated that I did not do well on my final and I asked him how could I get a failing grade from one bad test and

I was an A student. He stated that the final test was worth a large percent of the overall class grade. Then he stated that he would not mind showing me my test and that we could discuss it more in detail in person. I agreed because at that point I could not believe that I failed my exam. He asked for my address so that he could pick me up because I did not drive at the time. He met me outside of my house and I was very eager to see my exam. He said that we could go to his place because he had prepared a meal for us to eat. I really did want to go anywhere with him because I was so upset about my grade. We arrived at his apartment and I felt very uneasy about being there because I did not know him very well. He started to set the table and we sat down to eat. Later, I requested to see my paper and he showed me a paper full of red marks but it still was not clear to me how I failed my exam.

It did not make sense to me and he said that I could make the grade up if I wanted to. He started to walk towards me and placed his hands on my face and began to kiss me on my lips. I tried to pull away because I was starting to feel afraid of him. He walked towards his front door and removed the key that was in the door and looked at me in a strange way. He began to walk towards me and I asked him what he was doing. He told me that he wanted to make love to me and I asked him to please take me home because I did want him to touch me. He smiled in my face and grabbed me and directed me into his bedroom. He told me that I was not going to leave until he made love to me. My heart began to beat so fast because I was so afraid of what was going to happen to me. He told me to remove my clothes or he would do it himself. He forced me onto the bed and told me to stop fighting it because it was going to happen. He started to remove his clothes and I asked him if I could go to the bathroom. He told me yes and then showed me where it was located. He stood outside of the bathroom while I was trying to close the door. He opened the door and told me that I needed to crack the door and not shut it all the way. I started to cry and beg him to leave me alone. He just kept quiet and continued to look me up and down with his eyes. I went into the bathroom to see if there was a window that I could escape from but I was not able to do anything with him standing outside of the bathroom door. Finally, he said that I needed to come out of the bathroom and go into the bedroom with him. I hesitated for a while but I was running out of excuses. We went back into the bedroom and he told me to take off my clothes in a very angry voice. I sat on the bed and continued to tell him that I did not want him. He did not reply. I told him that I did not use any birth control and did not want to get pregnant. He never said a word but he continued to take off his clothes.

I finally removed my clothes as I began to cry. I was so angry, scared and confused. He pushed me back on the bed and climbed on top of me. I wanted to die right then so that it would be all over. I hated him breathing in my face while on top of me. He instructed me to open my legs and I began to fight him. He grabbed my hands and opened my legs with his legs and told me that I needed to stop fighting him. I stated that I did not want to get pregnant and begged him to please use a condom. I did not want to get a disease from him but he refused to stop. He forced himself inside of me and began to have sex with me. I refused to move my body but it did not make a difference to him. He continued to rape me over and over until he felt satisfied. Once I thought he was asleep I tried to leave but the door could not be opened without a key. I could not use his phone because he disconnected it from the wall. I had to stay there all night and I knew my dad would be wondering where I was because I did not call him. It was morning time and he told me that he was going to take me home. He told me to go take a shower and I pretended to wash myself. I did not want to wash away the evidence that I had been raped by my college teacher. He dropped me off one block from where I lived and pulled off in his car. I cried all the way home and as I thought, my dad was sitting on the porch waiting for my return. I ran past him and he followed me into the house.

When I was 21 years old I got pregnant by the man and I was so afraid to tell my dad because I was still living at home, working, and going to college. My dad pulled a gun out on the man several months ago and barred him from our home. Later, I told my dad that I was pregnant and he requested to speak to the man about the matter. The man begged me day in and day out to get an abortion because he was not ready for kids. He told me that if I did not get an abortion he would leave me and disappear somewhere in California so that I would have to raise the baby by myself. He was getting on my nerves so I agreed to get the abortion. We went to have the procedure done and I was told during an exam that I was too far to have it done. I knew that it could not be true so I told the nurse I was not far and she recommended that I have a sonogram done to verify how far I was in my pregnancy. The stomach measurement stated that I was measuring more weeks then I was supposed to be. My sonogram verified that I was not too far to have the abortion. After the procedure, the doctor said that I started to bleed badly which required them to give me a needle in both my thighs to stop the bleeding instantly. I was so scared that I was going to die on the table and I prayed for God to forgive me.

Experimenting with Life

One summer I caught the train to visit family in New Jersey. It was then that I was introduced to smoking marijuana that was laced with animal tranquilizer. I was 22 years old and had never experienced that kind of feeling before. I felt like I was moving in slow motion and I began to panic and act crazy. I thought that I had driven my car and I kept asking everyone where my car was and they told me that I did not drive. I remember going into the grocery store and feeling as though everyone was looking at me and talking about me. I wanted that feeling to stop so that I could feel normal again. I was told several times to calm down and that everything would be okay. I thought about what I had done and felt like it was going to impact my ability to get my teaching job if I were to fail my drug test. It was hard to stop thinking about not getting a job all because I wanted to experiment with a drug I knew nothing about or how it would affect me. I hated the way I was feeling and wanted it to all go away. Every time I tried to move or even talk it was in slow motion and it got on my nerves. I told myself that I never wanted to try this drug again.

Finally, hours went by and I could think straight again but I could tell I was not back to my normal self completely. I could not wait to get back home to Maryland and leave all the bad side effects behind. It was a Friday and I was scheduled to return home on Sunday. The drug was still affecting me on Saturday and all I wanted to do was cry out for help to make it stop. I made it back home safely with my thoughts and issues all behind me. I knew that I never wanted to try that drug again in my life. I was scheduled to report to the city location on Monday morning for my interview. I tried not to think about my terrible weekend experience and focus on my interview. I ended up getting the job and was not required to take a drug test. I thanked God for helping me pull through and decided to never try that drug again!

Later, I found out the man had another baby on the way the same time that I was pregnant and the child was born at 7 months with under-developed lungs and died. He was not who I thought he was. One day we were riding in his car when we got pulled over. When the police officer asked him what was wrong, he told them the car was stalling. It was also determined at that time that the car was not even registered to him. Later, I found out that the car had been registered in his wife's name who I knew nothing about. Can you imagine how messed up in the head I was? He tried to convince me that he had been separated for several years but I did not want to hear it or even believe him. Up and to this point, I had been dating a married man for about 4 years and didn't even know it. I could not believe I wanted to poison my dad one day because he kept getting in the way of our relationship. I had planned to poison my father and get him out of my business for good. Thank God, I did not go through with it. Dad knew what he was seeing and that I was not meant to be with this man.

I made it through that issue only to find out that he was a cheater. I went to his apartment while he was not there and saw an empty douche bottle in the bathroom trash can and it did not belong to me. When I questioned him about it he stated that he had let his brother use his apartment. I might be young but I am not stupid.

I was on my way to my GYN appointment and after my exam the nurse told me that I had a sexually transmitted disease. I asked her if I got it from a dirty toilet seat. She told me that it was from having intercourse with a person who was not clean. I told her that I only had intercourse with one person. The nurse said then my partner must have been with someone else because I was infected. I was enraged. This had never been an issue before! The nurse gave me some large white pills to take and also gave me some to give to my partner. I was told that he needed to take them or I would get infected again. All I could think about on the drive home was how dirty I felt. When I pulled up in front my door he was sitting in his car. He followed me into the house and asked me how my doctor's appointment went. I was so mad that I told him everything went fine. He looked at me as if it were not possible for everything to go well at my appointment. Several days went by and he never tried to have intercourse with me and I knew why. Finally, he asked me again if my appointment went well. I told him that he was a low down dirty dog for not being a man and telling me that he had infected me so that I could get treated.

I threw the pills at him and told him what was up with me. He told me that he would take the pills but denied that he was a cheater. Unbelievably, he infected me three more times and I was so done. I was blinded by what I thought was love, but I needed to get away before I contracted something pills would not be able to take away.

I was so distracted by my feelings for this older man whom I had fallen in love with, but I was determined to end the relationship for real this time. My dad and my sister were asleep in the house and I went into the kitchen to grab a knife. I sat at the kitchen table and wrote a letter to the man telling him how much he had hurt me and that it was his fault that I was going to kill myself. I put the note in my pocket so that it could be found after my death. I left the house around 12 midnight and walked towards a street named Green Mount Avenue. After a while I stopped and pulled out my knife so that I could cut my wrist open and quickly bleed to death. As I was trying to cut myself a stranger pulled up beside me in a car and asked me if I was okay. I was so scared that I dropped my knife and ran all the way to my dad's friend house that was in the area. I arrived at her house in tears and my body was shaking as if I was out of my mind. I explained to her what had happened and she told me to never let a man make me feel like I did not want to live because I was a very special person. She also told me that the pain I was feeling would go away and I would not feel that way forever. I believed every word she said to me and that is what saved my life.

I guess love can make you do some foolish things. I found out that I was pregnant again by the same man and I was now 26 years old. I had received my B.S. degree in Business Management and I had a good paying job. I told the man that he could do his own thing because I would not get another abortion. He stayed away from me until I was 7 months pregnant and then he started to come see me. I had made up my mind that I did not need him in my life because he had hurt me so many times.

I was still at home with my dad and my sister so that my dad could enjoy his retirement and not pay any bills.

My dad meant the world to me and I wanted him to enjoy life without financial problems. I went into labor early one morning while doing my laundry. My dad told my sister to take me to the hospital because I was in a lot of pain. We arrived at the hospital and I was seen right away. I was told that I was 2 cm and I needed to try to walk for at least an hour. I returned after my walk and as I was being checked by the doctor the curtain opened and there was my baby's father looking at me. I felt something wet and I was told that my water had broken and I was 4 cm. I asked him who called him and he said that my dad contacted him. I had nothing to say about it. Hours later my little girl was born and I was so glad to see her. She was so beautiful and I knew then that my life would never be the same. It was time to fill out the birth certificate document and my friend had no problem filling out his portion. I reviewed the document and realized that he was about 15 years older than I was. I was so surprised because he did not look his age at all. I was in total shock. He left the hospital and the nurse came to take my baby girl for observation. I t was getting late and my baby had not been returned to me so I called the nurse. I was told that she had yellow jaundice and needed to stay in the nursery under a light to help lower her levels. It was day three and I had to be released according to the health insurance regulations. I asked when my baby could be released and I was told that her levels were still too high to be released. On day 5 I received a phone call from the hospital to let me know that my baby was ready to come home.

On day 23, two days before Christmas, the baby's father showed up to tell me that I had given him such a beautiful child but that he was not ready to be a father and was breaking off our relationship. I said to him "really?!" He had not been around for a while so I was not worried about him leaving me. I was financially stable and I had enough love for our child for the both of us.

One evening I was over my baby's father's house and he was acting very strange. My sister was babysitting and was trying to contact me on his house phone. The next morning the house phone rang and my friend answered the phone and stated the name of a hospital aloud. The look on his face told me that something was wrong. He hung up the phone and started to get dressed and I left to go get my baby. I felt like something was seriously wrong but he would not say what it was. I went home and I called the hospital to inquire about a patient with the same last name as my friend. I was told that the patient was in a serious but stable condition. I began to wonder if this person was his son. Hours later my friend came to my house and I told him that I already knew that he had a child that he never told me about. The child was 22 years old and had been shot 6 times the same night I was over his house but he had turned the phone off because I was visiting. Wow! another issue to deal with.

My daughter was about 4 months old when I learned that my friend's son had died. He did not invite me to the funeral or even mention our daughter in the obituary. I sat outside of the church where the funeral was being held and watched him get out of the limo with his family. I paid a junky $10 to go get me an obituary and another $10 to give it to me. As I began to read the obituary I noticed that my friend had three other children other than our daughter who was not even mentioned and I began to cry. I never told him what I had done because I was so hurt that he was not letting his mom, sisters or brother know that she was born.

My baby was now 7 months old and her dad was trying to bond with her but all she would do is cry because she did not know him. My friend hid our baby from his entire family until she was 7 months old. He finally introduced us to his mother and she said that my daughter looked like the rest of the children and I knew what she meant. His mom did not like me at first because she thought I was going to give him a lot of babies and keep him financially burdened. Later she told me that I needed to take her son to court to get financial help. She said that I was a smart young lady who was trying to do right by him and my child but I should not let him off easy. We became very good friends and I made sure that she saw her grandchild as often as I could. We loved each other very much.

Christmas was coming and I wanted to make sure that my child had everything she wanted. She was 3 years old and such a very loving child. I was 28 years old and I took a part time job at McDonalds so that I could have extra money. My daughter had a wonderful Christmas and I even bought her dad some ties and a robe from the both of us. He was such a butthead because he didn't even bother to buy myself or our daughter a gift and instead of being grateful for the gifts we gave him, he told me he did not need any ties and that I should take the robe back to the store. I was so pissed off about his ungratefulness that I gave the items to my dad. I told him to leave and never come back.

I prayed to God that he would take away my pain so that I could heal and move on with my life. Several months went by and I was starting to heal with my daughter's father in and out of my life keeping me unbalanced. One day he came to me and asked me to marry him. By then my heart was so cold and I did not trust him at all. I knew that it was not worth me opening myself back up to him after healing from all the pain he put me through. I had matured and realized that I needed an honest man in my life, not someone who was going to cheat on me, therefore I could never love him the same way I once did. My broken heart and bad memories over powered the love that I once had for him. Everything I went through caused me to never trust him again.

The Grass Looked Greener

I started a friendship with a co-worker and he wanted to start dating. I explained to him that I was not interested in a relationship at the time because I had recently ended a 12-year relationship with my daughter's father. He said that he understood. He continued to have short conversations with me during work hours. He appeared to be very kind, but I refrained from thinking anything of it because I was still messed up in my head from all that I had been through in my past relationship. I remember asking him why he had so many keys on his keychain. He told me that he sold cars as his personal business. He always smelled so fresh and clean and had a million-dollar smile. I enjoyed our daily conversations and looked forward to seeing his nice smile. One day he offered to take me dinner and I told him maybe one day we could make that happen. At that point in my life I knew that I needed to remain level headed and raise my daughter.

The Scare of My Life

I was on my way to work one evening with the intentions of putting in my 2-week notice of resignation. I parked my car in the parking lot and went into McDonalds to work for a few hours. I was the closing manager for that evening. I noticed that the store manager was dressed in uniform and that the security camera was not connected. I asked the manager what was going on and he said not to worry because he was going to take care of it. He asked if I could work the drive thru window until the cashier arrived. I looked up at the clock and it was around 8:00 p.m. I headed towards the drive thru area and put on my headphones to take an order. I heard the alarm going off and I assumed that someone opened the back door before turning off the alarm to take out the trash. I had completed my first order and closed the cash register and I felt something nudging me in my hip. I thought it was one of the managers playing around with me so I said, "stop." The force was even more intense so I looked up to see who it was and it was a stranger. He was holding a gun to my head and told me to go with him. He was using me as his shield because the police were in the lobby waiting for him. He had just robbed the store and ran in the back area where I was working. As we walked out from the room I could see the store manager at the counter looking at me. The police officer had his weapon pointed towards us and instructed the robber to let me go. The robber told the police that he had nothing to lose and he continued to use me as his shield while we walked towards the exit door. My mind was all over the place and I thought that it was just a bad dream. I remembered that I had arrived at work at 8pm and it was now 9pm. The robber told me to walk faster and when I told him that I couldn't he hit me with the gun in my neck. I started to move much faster and as we were running down the street I fell on the ground. I laid there as if I was unconscious hoping that he would leave me but instead he picked me up off the ground and drug me into a dark alley. I was so scared to see that we were heading towards a vehicle. He opened the door and pushed me inside of the car. I just knew that I was going to die that night, as I thought to myself, "I have a 3-year-old daughter." The driver said that he was not going to get in trouble for any kidnapping charges and that the robber better get rid of me. The driver and the robber began to argue with each other about the matter. I felt like we were going to get killed in a car accident because the driver was riding through red lights without stopping and it appeared we were on the highway. I remember getting down on my knees, putting my arms around the robber's waist and begging him not to kill me because I had a 3-year-old daughter. He looked at me and said that he did not kill women. I was still afraid because the driver wanted me dead. I could tell by the way he looked at me and how he said to get rid of me.

They both continued to argue about what they should do about me being in the car. The driver said that he was not going to jail for any kidnapping charges. The robber said that he was going to take care of me and he told him to stop the car. The driver pulled the car over near the side walk and it was very dark on the street. The robber instructed the driver to go ahead and that he would catch up with him later. Before the driver got out of the car he stated, "Man, I mean it, you better take care of that girl." The robber told him that he would handle things. Then the driver left the scene.

The robber instructed me to get down on the floor and to stay down. I did exactly what he asked because I felt like he was going to shoot me in the back of my head and leave me for dead. I heard the car door slam and I jumped. Then I saw out of the corner of my eye a large duffle bag in the air. Later I heard the trunk of the car close and 3 gun shots one after another. I also heard some feet running away from the area where I was located. I was too afraid to get up and look because I did not know if the robber was gone. It was February, it was cold and I did not have a coat on. I finally decided to try to get some help because I was too cold just sitting in the car. I opened the door and looked around to try to figure out what I needed to do to get in a safe place. I saw a light on a porch so I drug my hurt leg up the steps and I knocked on the door. No one answered. I kept telling myself to remain calm so that no one would shut their door in my face.

I saw another light on a porch so I limped up the steps, leaned against the wall and knocked on the door. A little boy answered the door and I asked him if his mother was home. He said no then I asked if his father was home. He said, "Yes," so I asked the boy to get his father. The little boy yelled for his dad to come to the door as I requested. The dad asked who was at the door and I told him my name. The dad requested for me to come inside. I remember feeling very weak and lifeless at this point. I ended up passing out in the doorway of this stranger's home. When I regained consciousness, I saw several police officers and paramedics examining me and taking pictures of my injuries. Someone asked me if I had been raped and I shook my head no. I had thought to myself that my only fear was of my life being taken and not of me being raped. I was transported to the hospital and my dad was called. I remember hearing his voice on the phone and not being able to talk clear enough to explain to him what had happened to me. The nurse took the phone and told my dad what I had just experienced. I was so upset, scared and angry about the whole situation. All I wanted to do was go home and hold my little girl who almost lost her mother that night.

It was finally time to go home and I wanted to send a thank you letter to the people who helped me but I did not know where I was because it was so dark on the street and I had lost my glasses during my fall. A few days went by and I was contacted by an investigator who wanted to ask me questions about the robbery. I explained to him that I did not remember anything about the incident. He insisted on questioning me so I agreed to talk to him. He arrived at my home and my dad let him in the house. He told me that he wanted to ask me a few questions and that it would not take very long. The first question he asked me was if I remembered what the two men look like and I told him no. He showed me a large photo book and requested for me to look at some pictures. As he opened the book I looked down at the book and I saw both men's picture beside each other and I freaked out instantly. I could not deny that I did not see the men before because my reactions told on me. Then he showed me a revolver and asked me if I had ever seen that gun before. I answered yes and I was crying and shaking because I did not want to see the gun or those men ever again. My dad demanded for the investigator to leave because I was so upset. He apologized and he left.

I received a notice in the mail requesting for me to come to the police station to identify the robber and the driver in a line up. I was so afraid to go but I had no choice. I remember looking through a long piece of glass and seeing 8 men staring at me. I was told that they could not see me but it felt as though they could see me. I identified the men very easy and I was ready to go home.

A few months later I received a summons to appear in court to testify about the robbery and kidnapping. I was not looking forward to seeing those men again face to face. I was sitting outside of the court room waiting to be called.

A lawyer came to me and told me that the two men confessed to both crimes as soon as they learned that I was going to be testifying. I remember thanking God all the way home. I did receive a settlement from McDonalds for all that had happened to me, but nothing was better than me surviving the incident and regaining my mental health.

Later, my twin nieces' grandmother advised me to talk with a counselor and go through therapy so that I could receive some emotional healing. She referred me to a therapist and I continued to go regularly for several sessions. I remember telling my therapist how dirty I felt when I had to get on my knees and beg for my life. She reminded me that it may have saved my life. I was so out of sort at that time in my life. I could not go to work or even go outside because I thought that I would get kidnapped by strangers. I kept having nightmares about being choked and held at gun point. I didn't realize how much this situation had impacted my life and I was glad to be going to therapy to help me get through it.

I was ready for life to get back to normal so I decided to try and go back to work. I was on the escalator at the mall and I remember having a panic attack as I looked into the crowd of people. I remember thinking to myself that if a robbery took place where would I hide myself. I was ready to leave the Mall at once. I grabbed my daughter by the hand and began walking towards the exit that would take me out of the Mall. My daughter pulled her hand away from me because she saw a McDonalds and wanted to get some food. I started screaming like a crazy woman. I remember yelling to her come back here right now but I was too afraid to go into the McDonalds to get her. I was thinking that a robbery was going to take place any minute and we would be kidnapped. People were looking at me as if I had lost my mind. I ran over to my daughter and pulled her out of the McDonalds. My daughter began to cry and I picked her up and calmly told her that I would get her some food after we get into the car. She did not understand why I was so upset. I did not know how to explain my actions to her so I just kept on driving my car in silence.

The next time I met with my therapist I explained to her what had happened to me and she told me that I would have to go into a McDonalds and order something; this would be part of my healing process. I told her that I did not believe I could do it. I realized that I had to do it so that I could begin to heal in this area of my life. I realized that my life had to go on no matter how afraid I was about the incident reoccurring again. I finally managed to go into a McDonalds to order a small fry. I tried to act normal so that I did not draw any attention to myself. I immediately left the McDonalds as soon as I received my fries. As I was walking to my car I felt so relieved about what I had accomplished. It was time for my therapy to end and now I had to continue my healing process one day at a time.

My State employer was aware of what had happened to me and I had requested to take some leave from work. My twin sister worked in my same building, but on a different floor. My co-worker reached out to my sister to get my phone number and address so that he could visit me at home. One afternoon I heard a knock at my door and when I opened the door I was very surprised to see who was standing there. He handed me a card and said a few encouraging words to me that made my day. I thanked him for everything as he was leaving my house. He called me later in the week to check on me and see how I was doing. Three months had gone by and my friend wanted to know if I would go to dinner with him. I told him that I would go. He came to my house to pick me up. He opened the car door for me and handed me a rose.

I was very impressed about the royal treatment he had shown me. He made me feel very special. After dinner I arrived back home and I thanked my friend for a very lovely evening with him. He gave me his one and only charming smile and we gave each other a hug.

It was my first day back to work and I felt a little out of sort. I could focus just enough to work without interruptions but I was hoping that no one would question me about my absence because I was not ready to talk about it with anyone.

Three months had gone by since my kidnapping and my friend was getting closer to me but I wanted to take things slowly. I agreed to go out on another date with him and we had a really nice time. He took me back to his apartment and we ended up having unprotected sex. I was shocked that I went through with it because I didn't really know a lot about my friend and I was not on any birth control. I kept thinking how could I let this happen. I did tell him that I was not on any birth control but that did not change anything. I was angry at myself for not making him use a condom. What if I got a disease? I knew it was too late to even think about.

Believe it or not, I got pregnant. I knew I would have to tell my friend what was up, but when I told him he asked me if I was sure the baby was his since I had recently broken up with my daughter's father. I was so broken because I never thought he would say that to me. We agreed to get an abortion. I remember lying in my bed at home crying and thinking about all the drama in my life and how overwhelming it was. I begged my unborn child to forgive me but I knew that I could not go through with having a baby to a man that I barely even knew. I mean I couldn't even spell his last name. I was full of so many emotions and I knew it was my fault that I was in this position. My friend and I both took off work to go together to get the abortion. I told him not to talk about our relationship to any one on the job. Later when I returned to work someone approached me about me getting an abortion and I was so embarrassed. I knew that my friend had told someone. Later I approached him about it and he denied that he had told anyone. At that point, all I wanted to do was crawl up underneath a rock and die. It was too much for me to handle and I just wanted to turn back the clock. My friend and I did not communicate at all because of all the gossip that was going on in the office. I told myself that I just needed to go to work and stay to myself but it was so hard to do. We continued our relationship outside of the job and later I found another State job at another agency. I was so glad to move from that office. Now I could have a fresh start and get away from all the drama that was going on at my old job.

I was coming from the grocery store one evening and I was approached by a young man who asked me if I knew what time it was. I had just gotten out of my car and put my keys in my pocket so that I could carry my bags into the house. I looked at the watch on my arm and immediately felt a tug and pull on my purse. I realized at that moment that I was being robbed. The young man was trying to steal my purse from me. I tried holding on as long as I could but I felt like my finger was going to break from being pulled back so far so I let go. I stared at the man as he wrapped my purse around his arm and started to run away. I parted my lips to yell at him that I had no money inside my purse but I caught myself and ran into the house. I called the credit card company and then my bank to report my cards being stolen and have them cancelled. There was nothing else inside of my purse that was of any value. My dad had just told me about walking around with a lot of money in my purse. Thankfully, I had recently gone to the bank to make a deposit.

One Thanksgiving evening I was on my way to take care of some personal business. I remember looking at my dad and asking him if he was ok. He was not acting like himself and he was very quiet. I had a strange feeling about his behavior and I wanted to cancel my plans that day. My twin told me that she would be home and that my older sister would be arriving from New Jersey soon. I decided to go ahead and stick with my plans. Later when I arrived home I was greeted by my next-door neighbor. She told me that my dad had a stroke and was taken to the hospital via ambulance. My two sisters were still at the hospital so I told her she could go home and that I would wait at home with our kids. I kept pacing back and forth to the front door in anticipation of them coming home. Then I saw my neighbor who lived across the street looking out her door. She waved her hand to request me to come over to her house. I had a feeling that she just wanted to be nosey. I walked up her steps to find out what she wanted and she handed me a bag of cocaine. I looked at her in shock. I had already heard that she was a drug dealer in our area. She closed my hand and told me that I could pay her later. I said ok and I walked back across the street to go back inside of the house. It was on that day that I turned into a cocaine addict with a $600 a week habit. My dealer got me caught in her web before I knew what was going on. I had to have it almost every day and night. I was on the desert real tough and it was controlling me. I had to pay her every two weeks for drugs she was allowing me to buy "on the arm", meaning I could get the drugs and pay her later for them. Sometimes I would be up all night cleaning and snorting cocaine. I was a recreational user so I never missed a day from work and I always made sure my child was taken care of.

My Dad was not doing too well and I was so afraid that he was going to die. He was in his 70's and did not seem to be getting any better. He was placed in a rehab facility and he was not very happy about it. I had to be the one who signed medical papers so that he could receive a feeding tube inside of his stomach. The stroke had caused him to have trouble swallowing his food and it was going into his lungs and he was choking on it. This was the worst thing I ever had to see my dad go through. He was already wheel chair bound and his speech was impaired, too. One weekend my Dad asked me to take him home because he needed to get away from the rehab place. I knew that I would not be able to take him to his house because it was not equipped for a person in a wheelchair. My friend overheard our conversation while he was visiting my Dad. Later he told me that my Dad could come to his house for the weekend. I was thrilled to have an opportunity to get my dad out of the facility so I agreed to let my friend take him for the weekend. That next weekend we went to pick my Dad up and we took him to my friend's house. There was plenty of room in his basement which also had an entrance that we could use to bring dad inside. My Dad was so happy and I got the training I needed to care for his feeding tube properly. It was time for Dad to get a shower and I asked him if he needed me to change his pants and he said shook his head no. I knew he was going to be embarrassed about me washing him. I told my Dad that I have seen male body parts before and because he was my Dad I could face him in a direction where I would not see his private area. Then I told him that he was going to get a bath because he has helped me out all my life and it was time for me to give back and support all of his needs. He started to shake his head and he had tears streaming down his face. Later, we both started to laugh about how I had to get him to cooperate.

It was time to take Dad back to the rehab center and as I promised I would visit him every day during my lunch hour. My Dad's roommate would always complain about my Dad getting special treatment. He told me and my sister that my Dad got a bath everyday but he did not. I felt sorry for him and I know that my Dad was getting great care because at the time my sister was a social worker and she worked at the rehab place that my Dad was housed in. Every time we would leave the rehab facility, my father would get sad and I knew it was killing him inside.

Nine months had gone by and we continued to visit Dad every day. One morning my Dad's girlfriend called to tell me that her sister had died and that she would be willing to care for my Dad in her home. I was so glad to hear her say that and I could not wait to tell Dad. I had the power of attorney over everything so I could remove Dad at any time. To see the smile on Dad's face when we told him that he would be going to stay at his girlfriend's house made a world of difference for us. He laughed and cried at the same time. My Dad was well taken care of and I had peace of mind. One night I received a call that my Dad had been taken to the hospital because he was having mini strokes and had also had a seizure. I arrived at the hospital to see my Dad. He was so weak and he did not say much at all. I hugged him and told him how much I loved him. He was stable enough to leave the hospital after a few days. He was never the same after that day, but I prayed for him to get better. I held my Dad's hand before I left the house and I noticed that his eyes were gray and transparent looking and I had never noticed that look before. I told my Dad that we would be ok and if he needed to rest we would be able to make it. He looked me straight in my eyes as if he knew what I was saying. He reached out for my hand and he squeezed it very tight as if he did not want to let go. I still felt his hand in my hand as I was going to my car. I did not understand what was going on but I had a strange feeling. I remember the doctor telling me that they could only keep him comfortable and I did not think he was going to get better. It was a Thursday and we had a terrible snow storm so I was not able to visit dad that Friday but my sister and I had made plans to visit dad on that Saturday. My friend had asked me to go with him while he took care of some business. I remember telling him that I needed to go see my dad and that my sister was probably waiting for me. He finally said to me "what is wrong with you today"? "All you keep talking about is going to see your dad and you see him all the time so I'm not sure why you keep saying it over and over." I was not aware that I had repeated myself so much. We returned to his house and I was about to call my sister to tell her that I was on my way but I noticed that the caller ID had showed 8 missed calls from my house. I immediately called home and my niece answered the phone. She said, "Auntie where have you been?" My mom has been trying to reach you because DAD DIED!!! I asked her "what did you say?" She repeated it again. I told her to put my sister on the phone and she said that she went over to the house where dad was. I hung up the phone and I called the house. One of the boarders answered the phone and I asked him was my Dad dead? He said, "Yes." I asked him what happened and he said that he did not know. I asked him if my sister was there. He said, yes, so I told him to tell her that I was on my way. I started to cry and my friend asked me what was wrong. I told him that I had to go see my Dad because he was dead. He told me that it was not true and that maybe the person I talked to did not really know the truth. I told him that he would not have said that if he did not know. We got into the car and all I could do was cry as I thought about how I took too long to go see my dad and now he was gone. We arrived at the house and could see the ambulance parked in the street. I jumped out of the car and ran the rest of the way to the house. I went into the house and I saw Dad was sitting in his wheel chair. I started to talk to dad as if he was still alive. I told him that it was ok for him to rest and I kneeled to hug him. I felt his legs and they were hard as a rock. I looked up at his face and it appeared to be falling and seemed a little disfigured. I asked the paramedic if my dad was dead and he ignored me. I told him that he was very rude and he still never said anything.

I could not get myself together because I did not want to accept the fact that my dad was dead. I remember thinking to myself how I had only seen something like this on TV and here I am watching them bring my dad out of the room on a stretcher inside of a long black body bag. I was in total shock! My Dad's girlfriend took me to a funeral home so that I could make my dad's funeral arrangements. I was 35 years old and had never done this before. I was now motherless and fatherless and I felt like I was in this world alone. I had just started my new job on a Wednesday and dad died on that Saturday. I had no idea that this day would turn out to be the last day of my dad's life. I began thinking about how eager I was that day to go and see my dad. My dad's girlfriend told me that before he died he was talking very clearly and he told her that Martha (my mother) and Horace (Dad's brother) were coming to get him, but they were both deceased. Dad was pointing to a corner in the bedroom but she didn't see anything. Dad asked her to sit down and he thanked her for all her help. He told her that she was a good woman. She said that after he said those things to her he looked so peaceful and relaxed. He just sat in his wheel chair while she was talking to a friend who had come to visit her. She told me that she heard dad take a deep breath and then he was quiet. Her friend said that she needed to check on dad because his breathing sounded very loud. She realized that dad had taken his last breath. She immediately called our house and told my sister that we should come because she believed my Dad had just slipped away from us. My sister was not sure what she meant by that so she went directly to the house and had my niece contact me.

All the arrangements had been made and it was time for the family to view Dad's body. My twin and I could not get past seeing the advertisement board with Dad's name on it. Seeing dads name listed on the board made it real for us. He was really gone. We both broke down but knew we had to get ourselves together before we went in to view dad's body. Once I looked at Dad I could not believe my eyes. He looked so young, handsome and at peace. This made us happy. I was glad to see him looking so peaceful.

The day of Dad's home going was so hard for me. I remember standing in the kitchen crying and I heard a voice say to me, "Stop crying because he has made it and you know what to do to see him again". I ran from the kitchen because I was afraid of what I heard and I never saw anyone in the kitchen with me. I never mentioned it to anyone because I knew it would have seemed as though I was crazy.

During the home-going service I held back my tears because I was relieved that Dad was not suffering anymore with his illness. The burial site took my emotions to another level because I knew this was it, our final goodbye. Dad served in the Army so he had a small ceremony where the American flag was folded neatly and given to the oldest child. I was so full of emotion having to leave my dad there in the casket at the burial site. They did not lower the casket in the ground until we left the premises.

Several days later, one Saturday morning I woke up early and started to iron my clothes and prepare to go see my Dad. I was in denial that morning because I truly believed I was going to his girlfriend's house to visit him. My friend asked me where I was going and when I told him that I was ironing my clothes so that I could go over to my Dad's girlfriend's house to visit him, my friend just looked at me. Suddenly, I realized that Dad was really gone and that I was not going to see him again on this earth. I broke down crying like a baby. My friend hugged me with so much compassion in his eyes.

Dad had been dead for about 7 weeks and I was having problems with breast pain so I made a doctor's appointment to find out what was going on with my breast. My twin sister went along with me for support. I remember stopping by my cousin's house one morning to get her to look at my swollen breast. She was a nurse and when I lifted my top to show her she looked very surprised. She agreed that I needed to go get checked out.

Once I arrived at the doctor's office I was asked to give a urine sample. I asked myself why would they need my urine when I am here to have my breast examined. Finally, the nurse returned to the room and asked me a series of questions. She said that I was pregnant and I asked her how I could be pregnant. The nurse replied she did not know. I was in complete shock because it was now March and my dad had died in February. They estimated that I was about 7 weeks pregnant and I realized that Dad had been dead for 5 weeks.

The news of me being pregnant was too much for me to handle at that moment. I returned to work but all I did was sit at my desk and look in the mirror and think about what I was just told. I was turning 35 years old soon and I was not planning to have another baby. My daughter was 9 years old and I could not imagine starting over again but abortion was not an option for me this time. I became very depressed because of all that I was dealing with. My dad had just recently passed and I find out that I'm pregnant, not married yet, and was probably going to be a single mom all over again. How was I going to explain the news to my friend? I was still trying to clear my head and accept the fact that I was pregnant. I knew I had to tell him since we didn't exactly plan to have a baby. After I got myself together, I finally told him that I was pregnant and that I was planning to keep the baby. He didn't have any children and he seemed undecided about the idea of having a baby. I was on birth control at the time but I believe with all of the stress and running back and forth taking care of my dad while he was ill caused me to miss taking my pills every day. My friend did not show much emotion regarding my pregnancy but I could tell that he was getting use to the idea of becoming a father. He purchased a very nice crib and made sure that I and the baby had everything we needed. One day he told me that he was going to name the baby. I was ok with it at first until he told me that he wanted to name our son Peter. I said what? And why? He pulled out the bible and began to tell me about things that Peter did in the bible. When I went to sleep, I realized that he was serious.

My friend and I had a cool relationship for about nine years and when my son turned two years old I moved out of my friend's house into my own place. We had a culture difference and I knew that we could not continue living that way. He was a great provider but he did very little bonding with our son. I always did things with my family and we rarely did family things together as parents. I never held it against him because that's how it was at the time. My friend was not happy about the way I left because he came home one Saturday evening and I had moved out. We had talked about it previously but I never gave a date or time to move out. I had been praying for God to send me a man of God who would be equally yoked with me and who would enjoy going to church with me to praise the Lord. Sometimes he would be wondering why I spent so much time in church. God told me one day that I was praying for a man of God but I was not a woman of God. That made me re-evaluate my lifestyle. God also told me that I had been living in the wilderness for 20 years and living my life the way I wanted to and that I should try to live my life according to His will. God asked me what I had to lose by trying to live my life according to His will. I began thinking about those things God had spoken to me all the time. Before I moved out, I even started sleeping in another room. I remember God saying to me you're still shacking up because he is not your husband. I began meditating on God's message to me and I really wanted to be in His grace for all the things he had brought me through.

I never felt lonely or incomplete when I moved into my own place. My friend told me that it was impossible for me to just shut myself off from having any relationships with him and he thought I may have been seeing someone else. I knew that it was not true so I continued to pray for God to keep me from going back to my old life style.

I had been praying for God to send me to a church where I could spiritually grow. One day I was at the traffic light at Frankford and Sinclair Lane and I heard a voice say look to your right. I looked and I saw a church sitting right there that I had never seen before. I had passed that area for about three years or more and never saw any church before. I went home that day and I told my twin sister and one of my older sister's I had found a church and that no matter how tired I was on Sunday I was going to go to that church. They asked me what the name of the church was and I said New Creation Christian Church. Both of my sisters said that they were going to go to the church with me. Sunday morning came and I called my sisters on the phone to see if they were still going to come. They both said they would meet me there. I drove up to the church and my son and I went in. I began experiencing a presence that I never felt before. I could feel something different happening to me even before I entered the sanctuary. I really can't explain it but all I know is that the Lord began to speak to me and He said to me," You asked me to send you somewhere so that you can spiritually grow so this is where you need to dwell". I knew that I would be attending the church because of the connection I felt that day.

I continued to worship at New Creation Christian Church; I developed my spiritual life and I started to grow in the Lord more. I wanted to join the choir because in the past I could really sing soprano but because of my past drug addiction I ruined my voice. The Lord referred me to the dance team but I really did not want to dance. I started to meet some very nice members at NCCC and I really felt welcome at the church. I remember my first time attending the church I saw a very handsome pastor who began to preach the word of God and what really touched my heart was when the pastor began to cry in front of the congregation. I realized that he was very serious about winning souls and salvation for his members. He would preach a message each Sunday that would convict me if I were not living right or if I was starting to backslide. This pastor stepped all over my feet with his real life, down to earth messages. I had no choice but to live right or I would have to leave with my head hanging down because the Lord would use him in such a way that I knew the messages were just for my hearing and understanding. I met a lady at the church that I really became close friends with and she treated me very nice all the time. I also met a man that was like a father to me and he was very special to me. The lady and I became so close that I introduced her to some of my family members. I remember one day the lady and I went to her brother's house because she needed to pick something up from his house. One night I had a dream that a man had kissed me on my lips but I could not see his face very clear. I prayed and said, God if a man kisses me on my lips he better be my husband because I could not imagine who the man could be. When the door opened I saw the face of the man that kissed me and I could not believe my eyes. It was the man I had kissed in my dream and I was surprised to see his face.

One day I was talking to one of the members, the son of the lady I had gotten close to, and we had planned to go bowling that Saturday. We had developed a close relationship and he was like a nephew to me. We came up with a saying that we would use with each other, "going my way" and we would lock our thumbs together to symbolize our saying. The day we planned to go bowling he called me to ask if his uncle could go along with us. I asked him who his uncle was and he told me that he was the man who played the drums. I fell onto my bed to keep myself from losing oxygen because I was breathing out of control. I remember looking at the drummer man and saying to myself he is serving the Lord and he is handsome too. I agreed that the drummer man could go bowling with us. Later I heard a knock at the door and when I opened the door, I saw a very tall handsome man looking at me. He told me his name and I could not take my eyes off him. We walked to the car and he opened the door for me and I sat in the front seat. When we arrived at the bowling alley I was concerned because I had never been bowling before. The drummer man explained to me how to hold the bowling ball and when he touched my hand to demonstrate, I felt the electricity flowing through my hand from his hand. It was amazing to even experience something like that just from his hand touching my hand. After that I realized that I needed to get me a fishing rod because I was going to catch me a live one. He was everything I was looking for; a man of God, handsome, honest, kind to my children and he loved my cooking. He was not trying to have sex with me either, even though we kissed, hugged and sometimes cuddled on the sofa. He was not disrespectful to me and we seemed to have a lot in common. We continued to date and got even closer.

Then it was time to meet his parents the true worshippers and God-fearing people. I told the drummer man that I did not think I was good enough to meet his parents. He knew I was afraid that they would question why their son would date a woman like me with 2 children of her own, a 13-year old daughter and a 4-year old son. They treated me very nice and I was so comfortable with our meeting. I told the drummer man that I wanted to keep our relationship private so that no one could have anything to say about us dating. He agreed with me. He proposed to me one day in the month of October and I declined because we both had too much baggage to enter marriage. I had never been married before and it would have been his second marriage. In January, he asked me again to marry him and I said yes. I asked him when would he want me to be his wife? He looked at the calendar and said "March". I asked him what date. He said the 23. I accepted that date and we began to plan for the short notice wedding. He got the marriage certificate and we picked out our rings. Everything was happening so fast and before I knew it my birthday, March 21st had approached us. I was awakened from my sleep when I heard a voice say to me "What is the day's date"? I sat up on my bed and said to myself it's my birthday. Then the voice said to me what is going to happen in two days. I thought about it and then I started to cry because I remembered that I wanted to get married to a man of God by the time I was 40 years old. I prayed that prayer when I was 10 years old and God reminded me that he did not forget.

Conclusion

I realized that all the pain and suffering, trials and tribulations that I went through from my childhood years and throughout my adult years were going to be a testimony for someone to see that God is a deliverer and He is always on time. My past experiences made me stronger and I am not ashamed of what I went through. One day I would tell my story to bring healing to others and give them hope that their life can get better. You can be healed! No matter what it looks like, never give up! Suicide is not an option or I would not have been able to tell my story.

No matter what I was going through I always prayed about it and my faith increased and that is what kept me going day by day. I pushed through the hard times, the bad choices I made and everything I went through. I realized God was waiting on me to make a change in my life and that releasing the skeletons in my closet would bring me healing.

He never left my side; I just had to be willing to live my life according to His will. I realized that I could help someone else believe in themselves by showing them that I am still standing, even with everything I went through. I am in my right mind. I have my health and my strength. One thing I know for sure is that praying really worked a miracle in my life.

CPSIA information can be obtained
at www.ICGtesting.com
Printed in the USA
LVHW01s1706061117
555223LV00002B/126/P